Adult Coloring Book

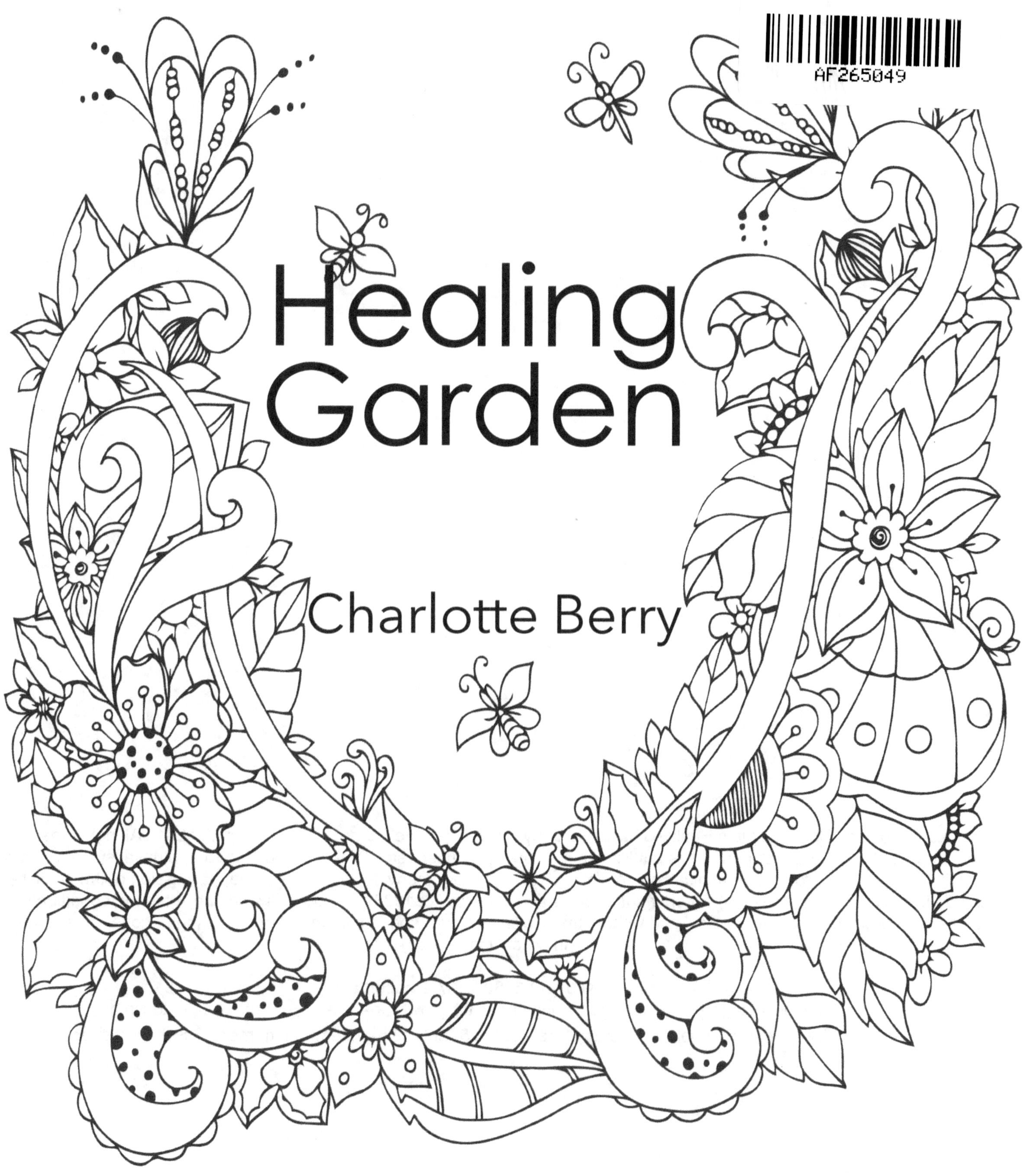

Healing Garden

Charlotte Berry

ISBN:978-0-6480768-7-2 paperback.
BIC Subject category: 1. Drawing-coloring books for grown-ups 2. Arts & Photography- techniques
3. Craft, hobbies- art 4. Self-help-art therapy & relaxation 5. Self-help-anger management. 6.Self-help-stress relief

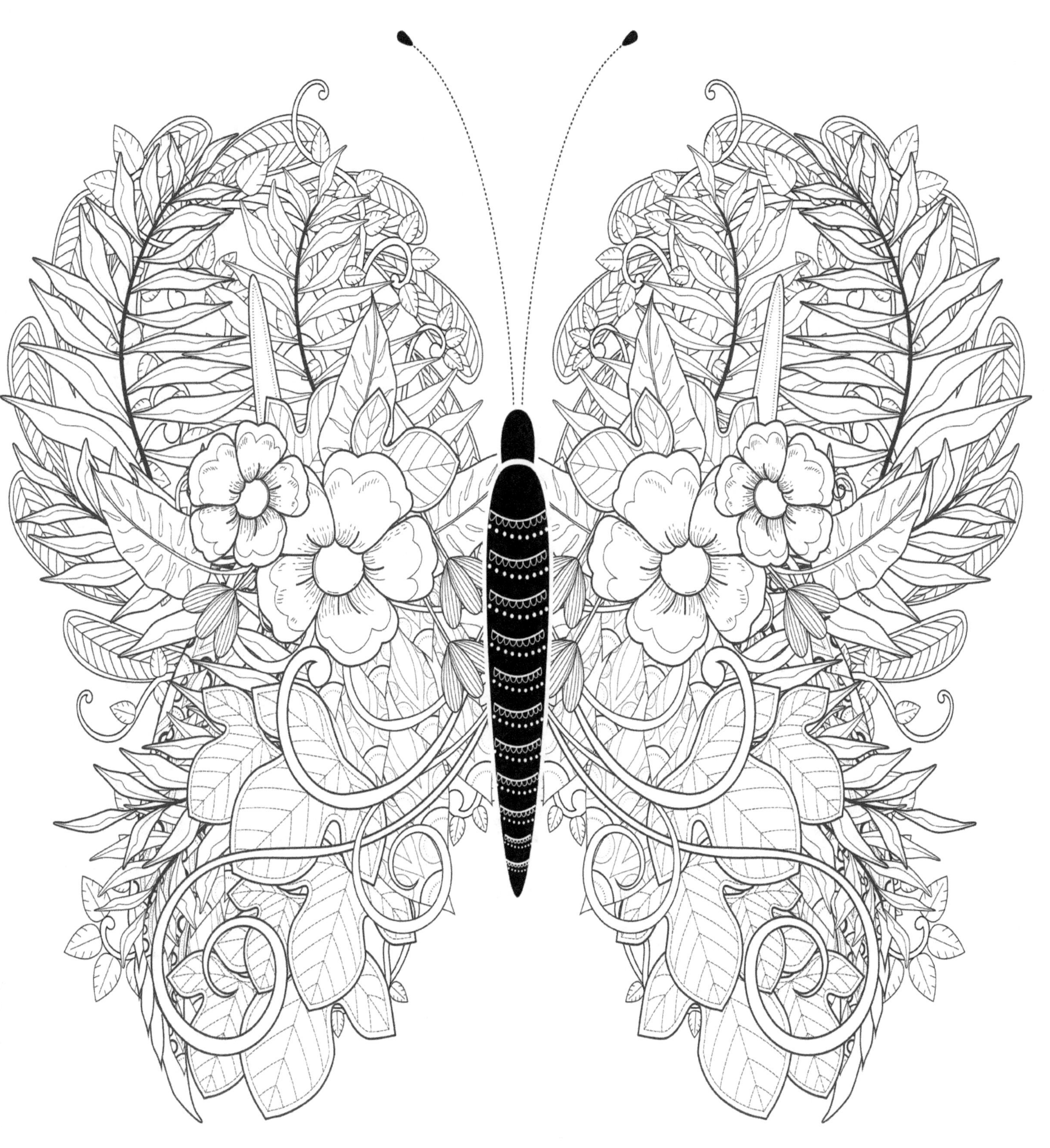

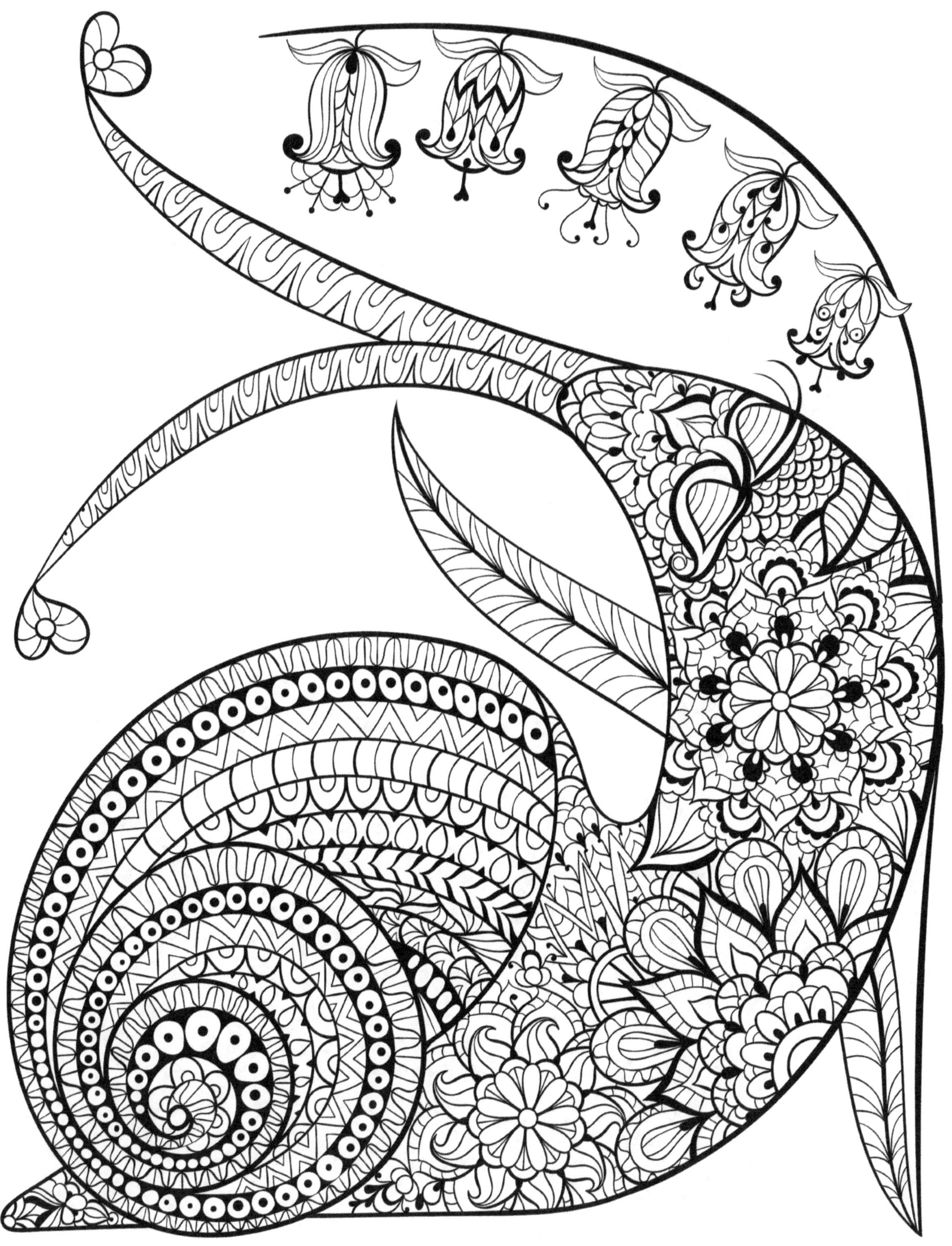

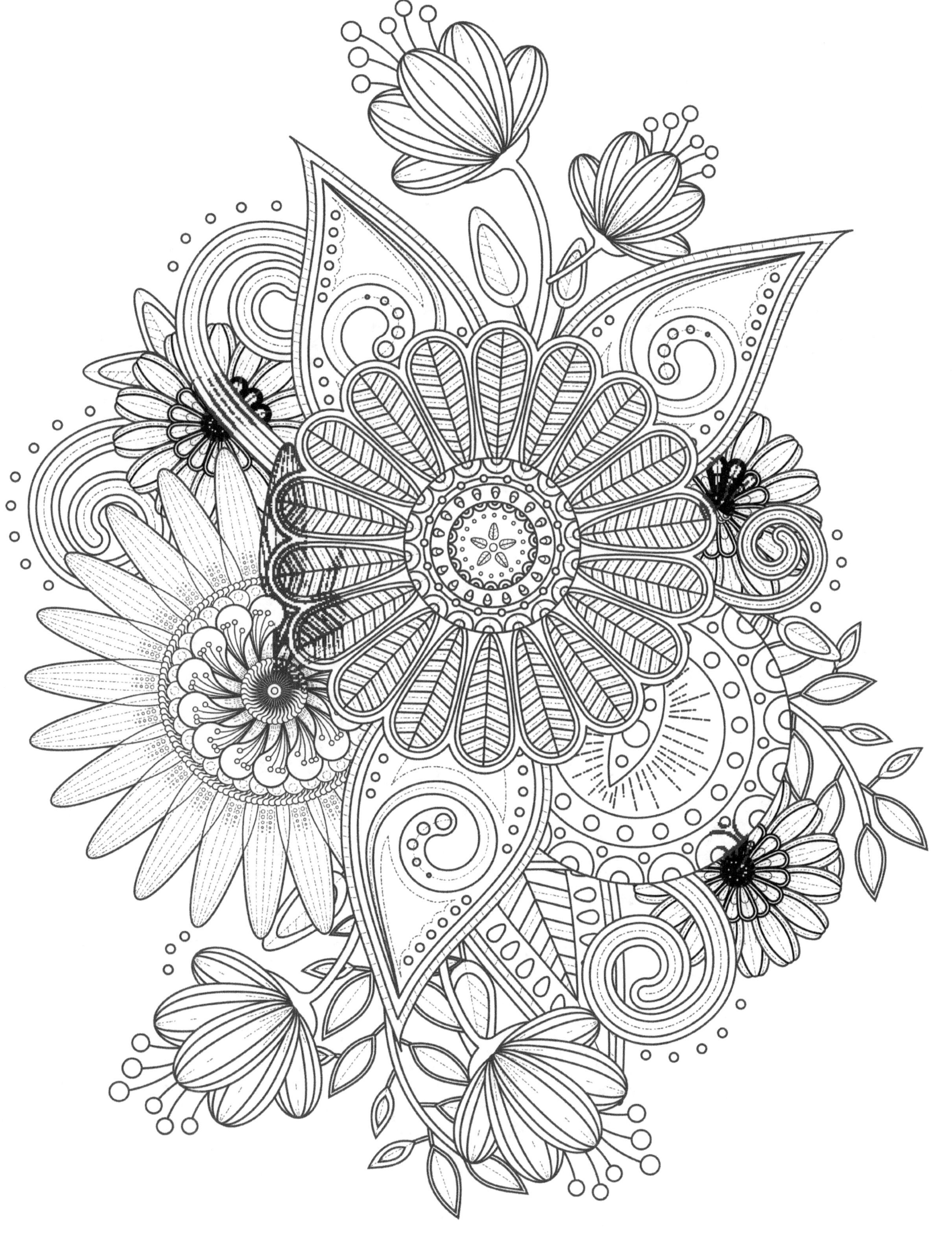

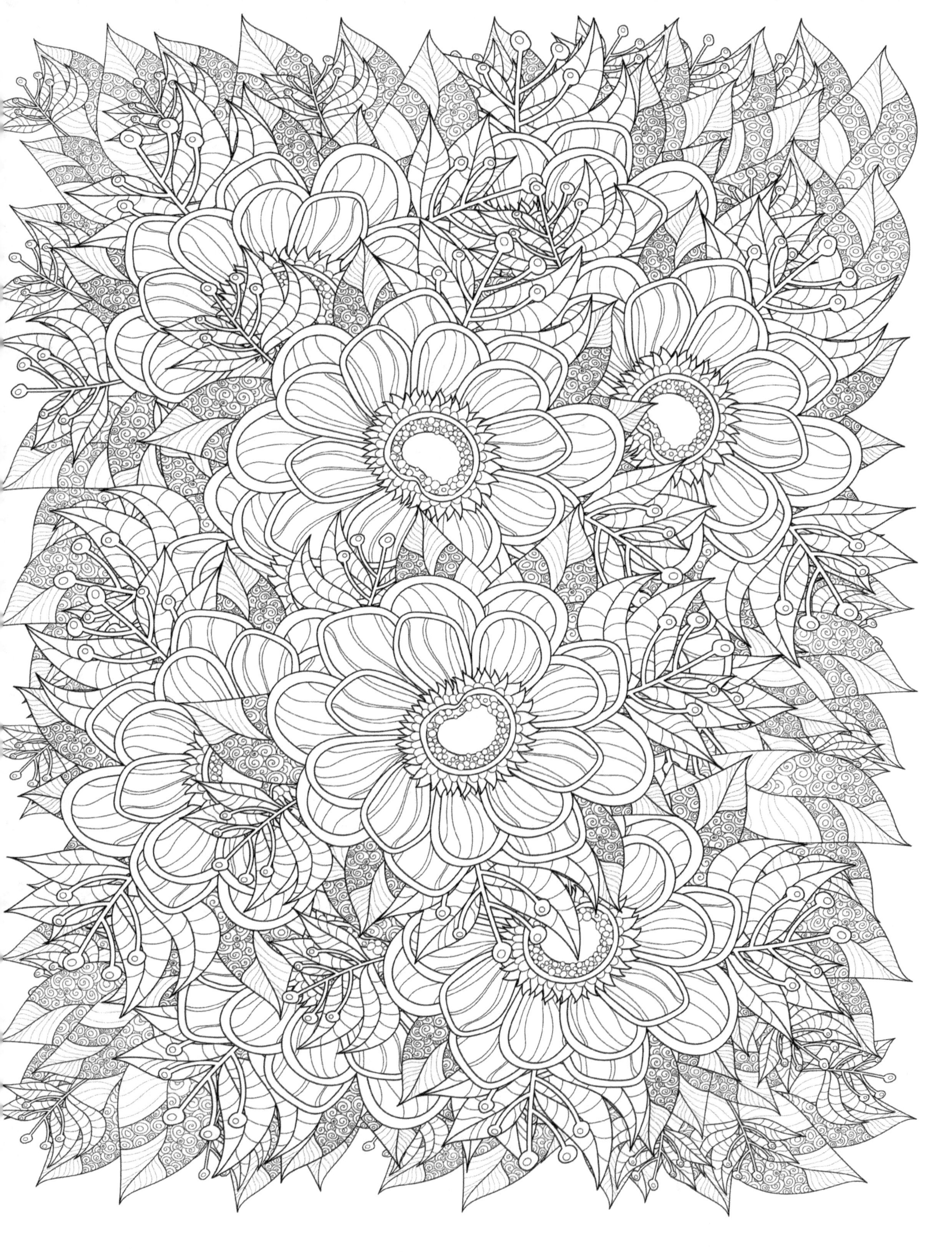

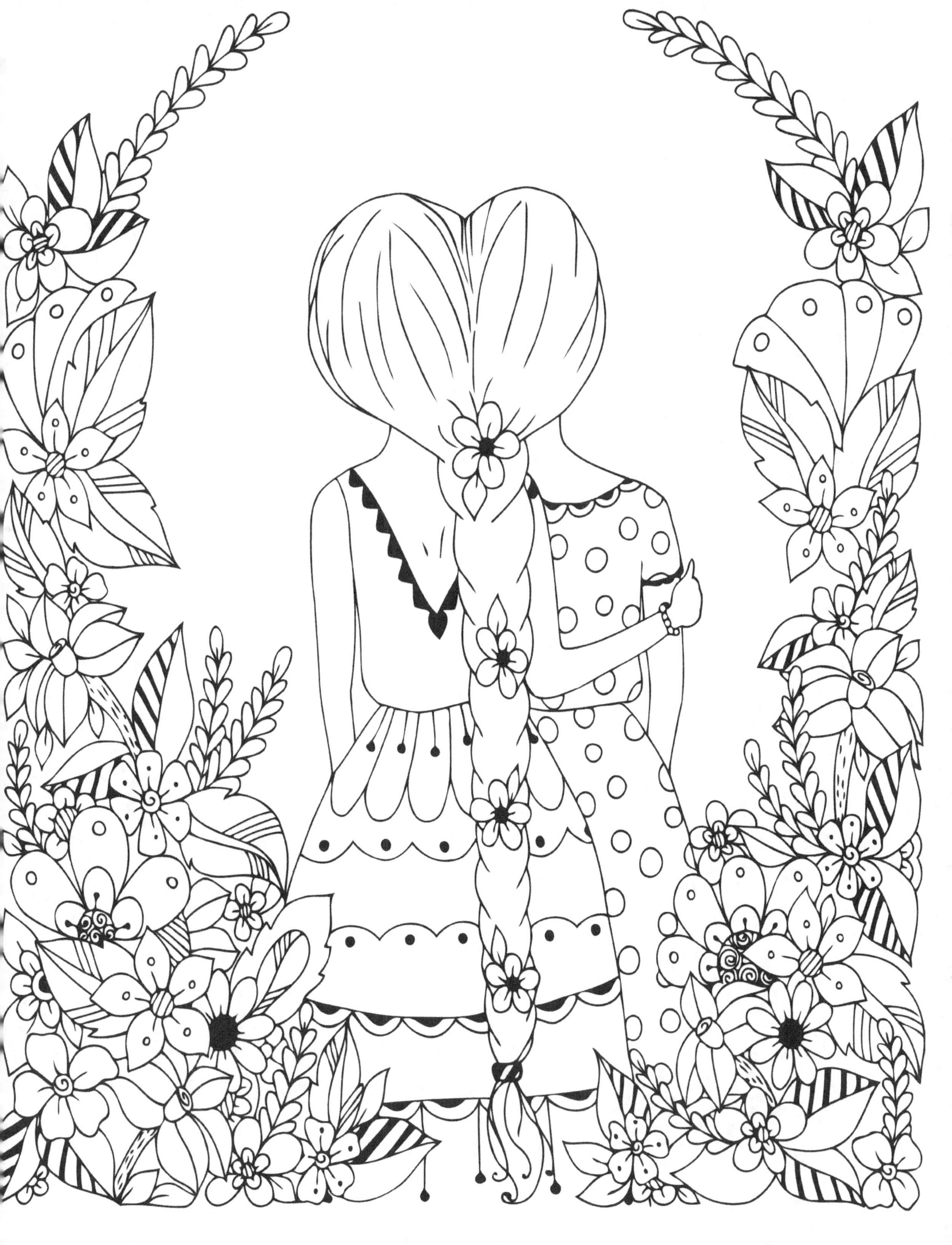

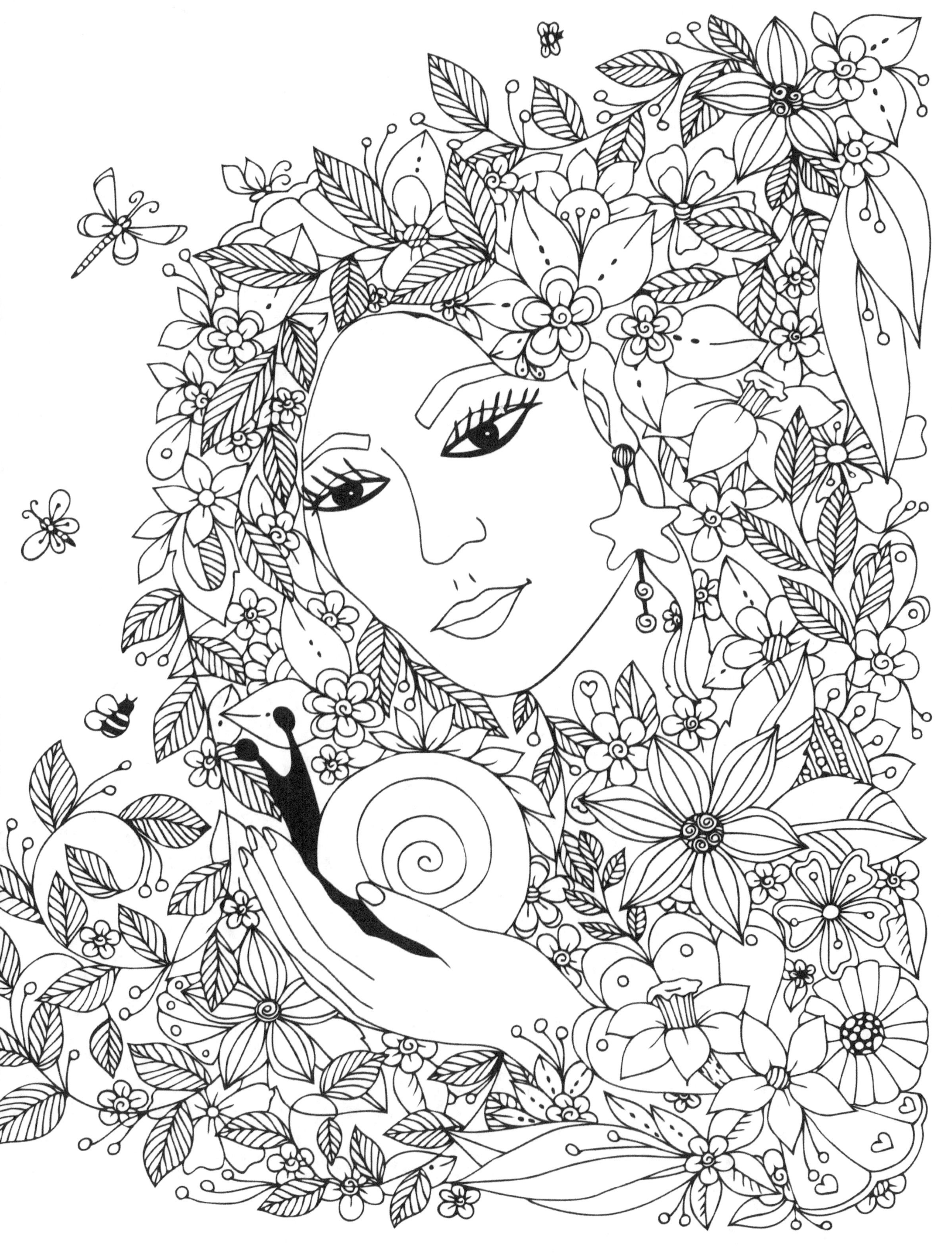

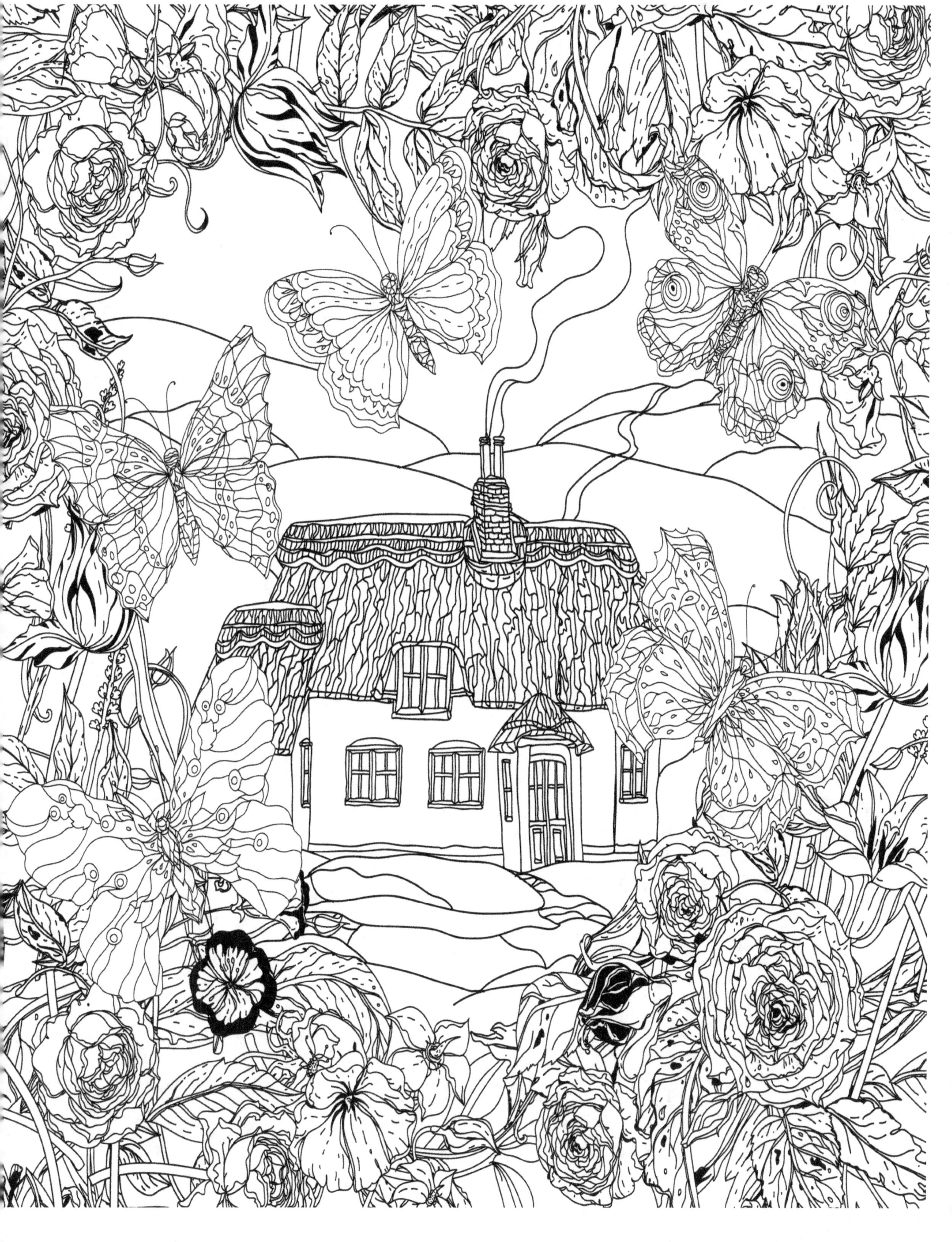

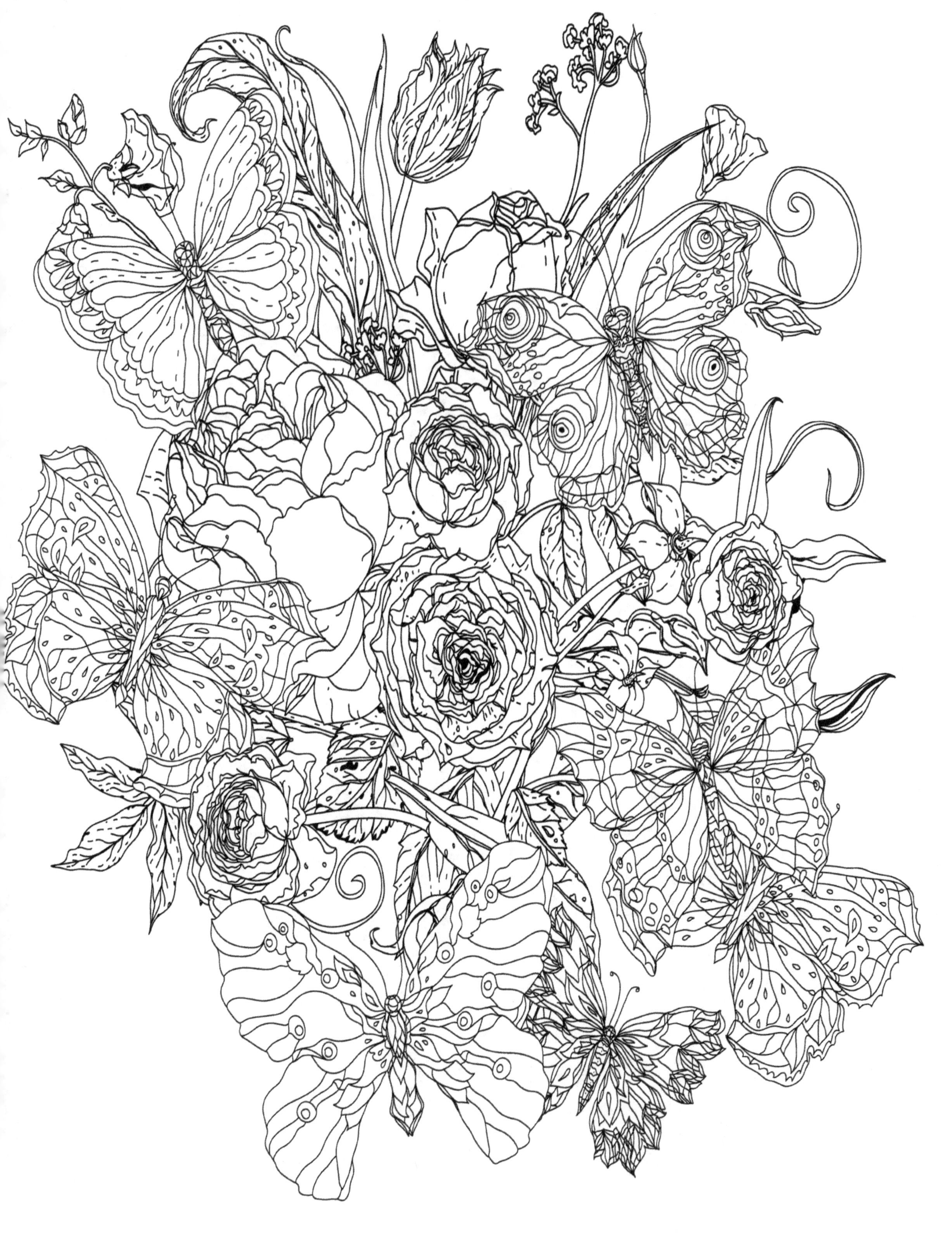

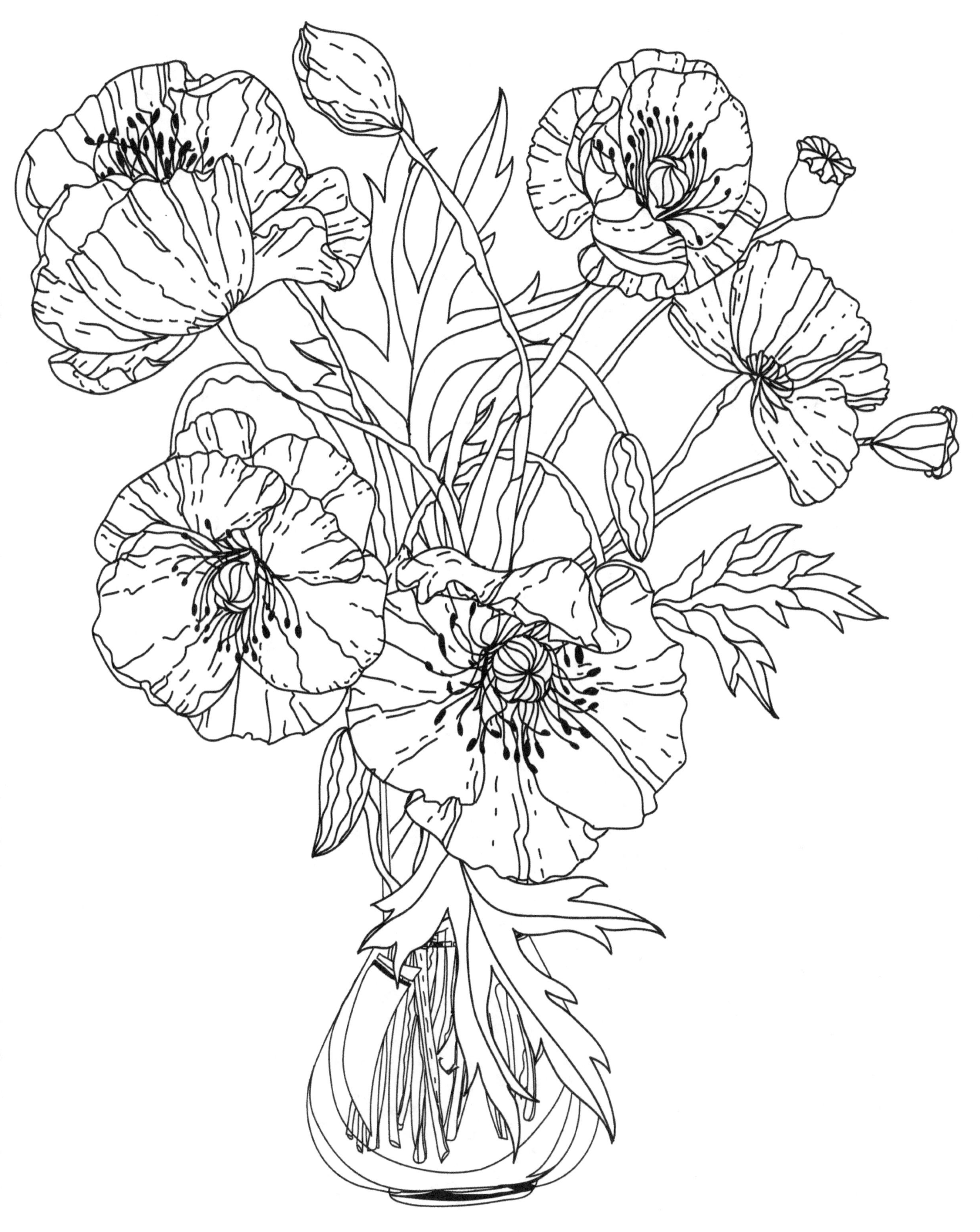

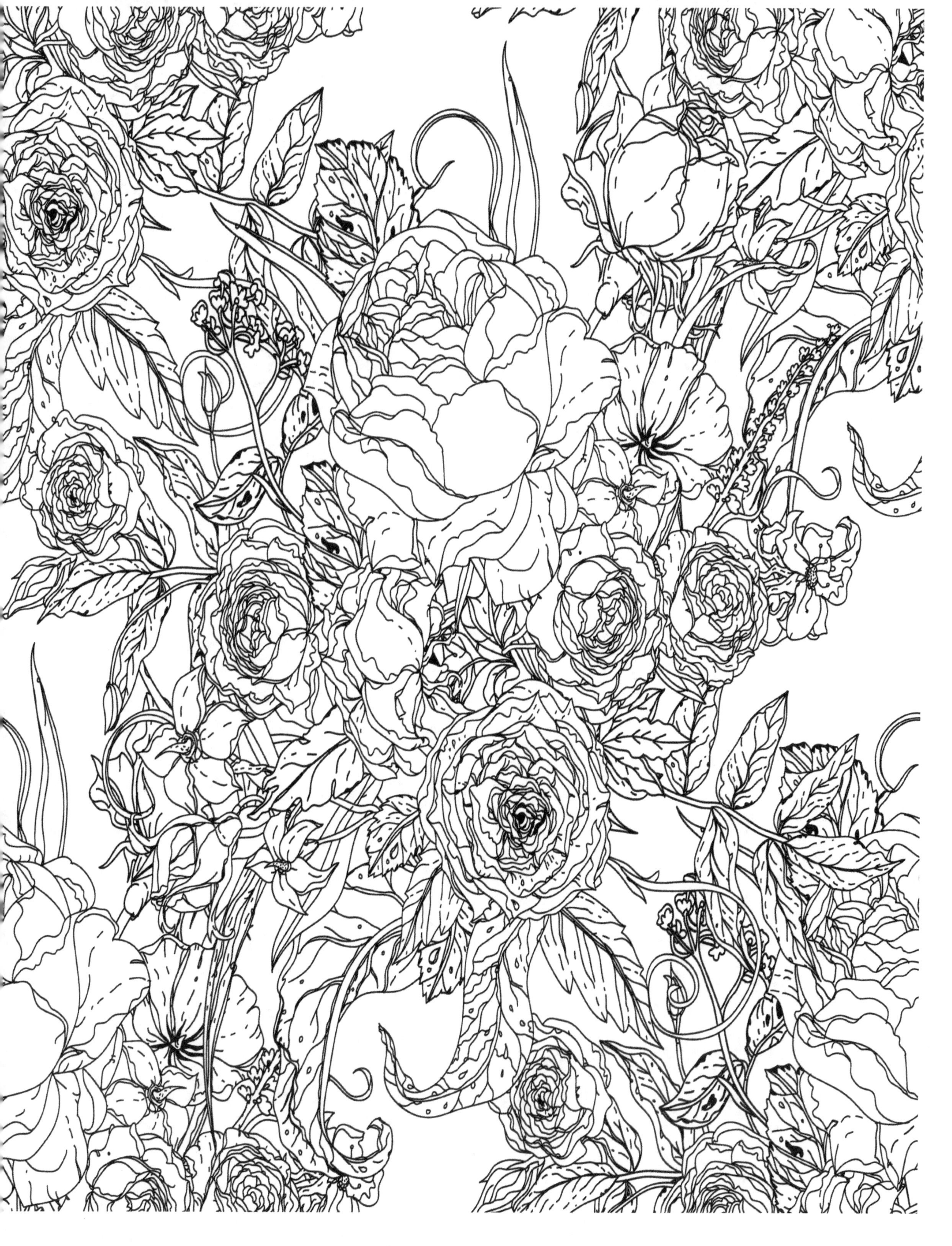

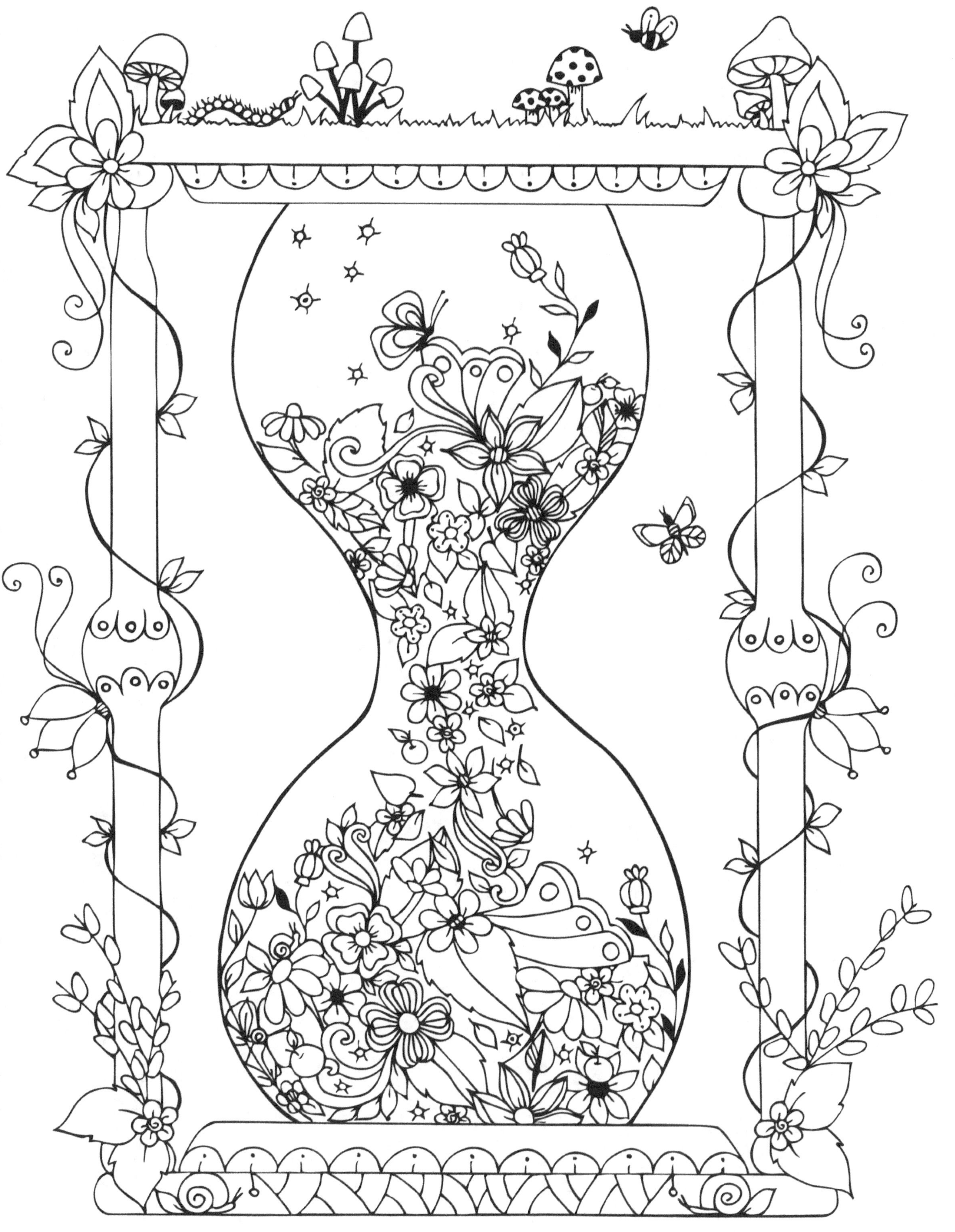

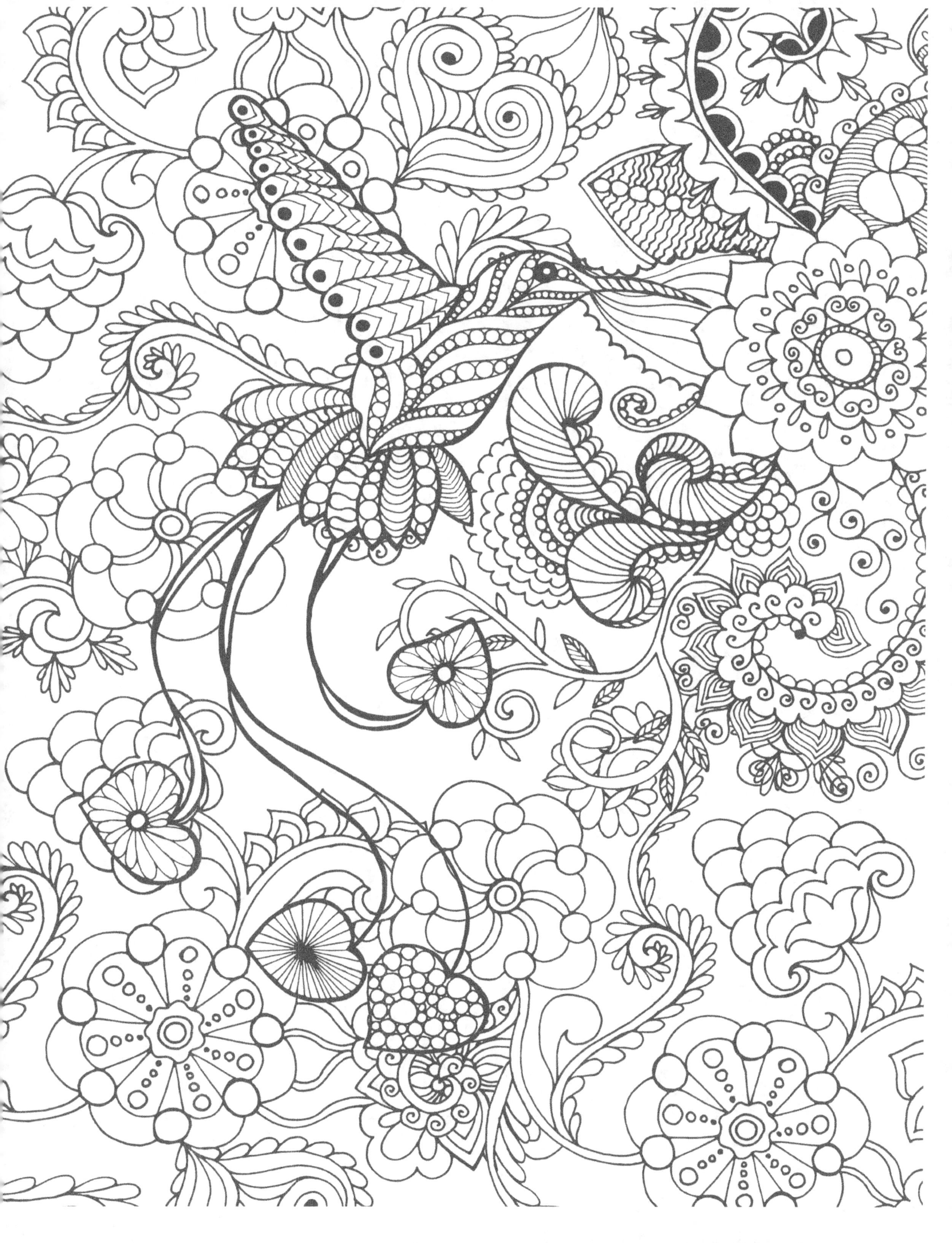

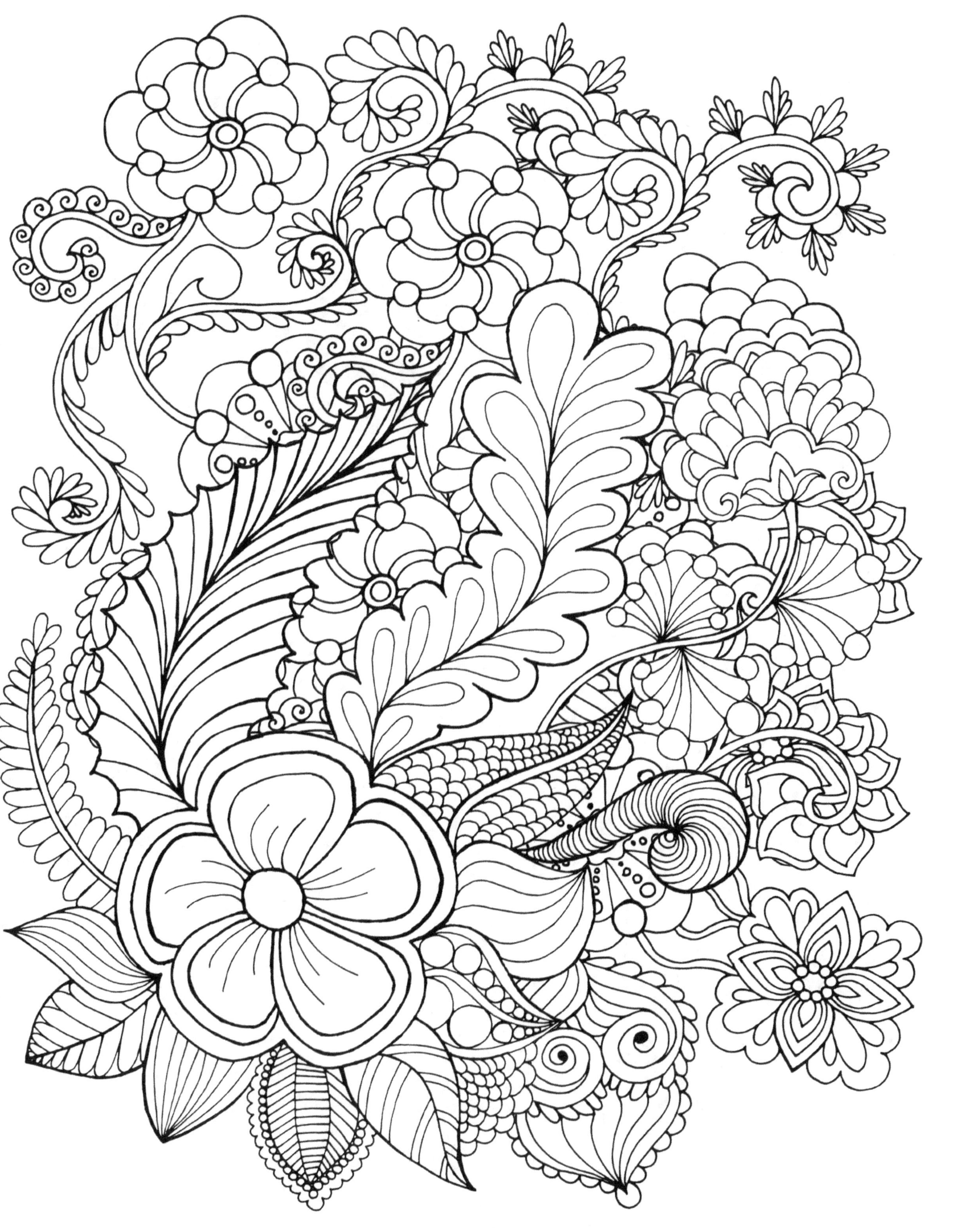

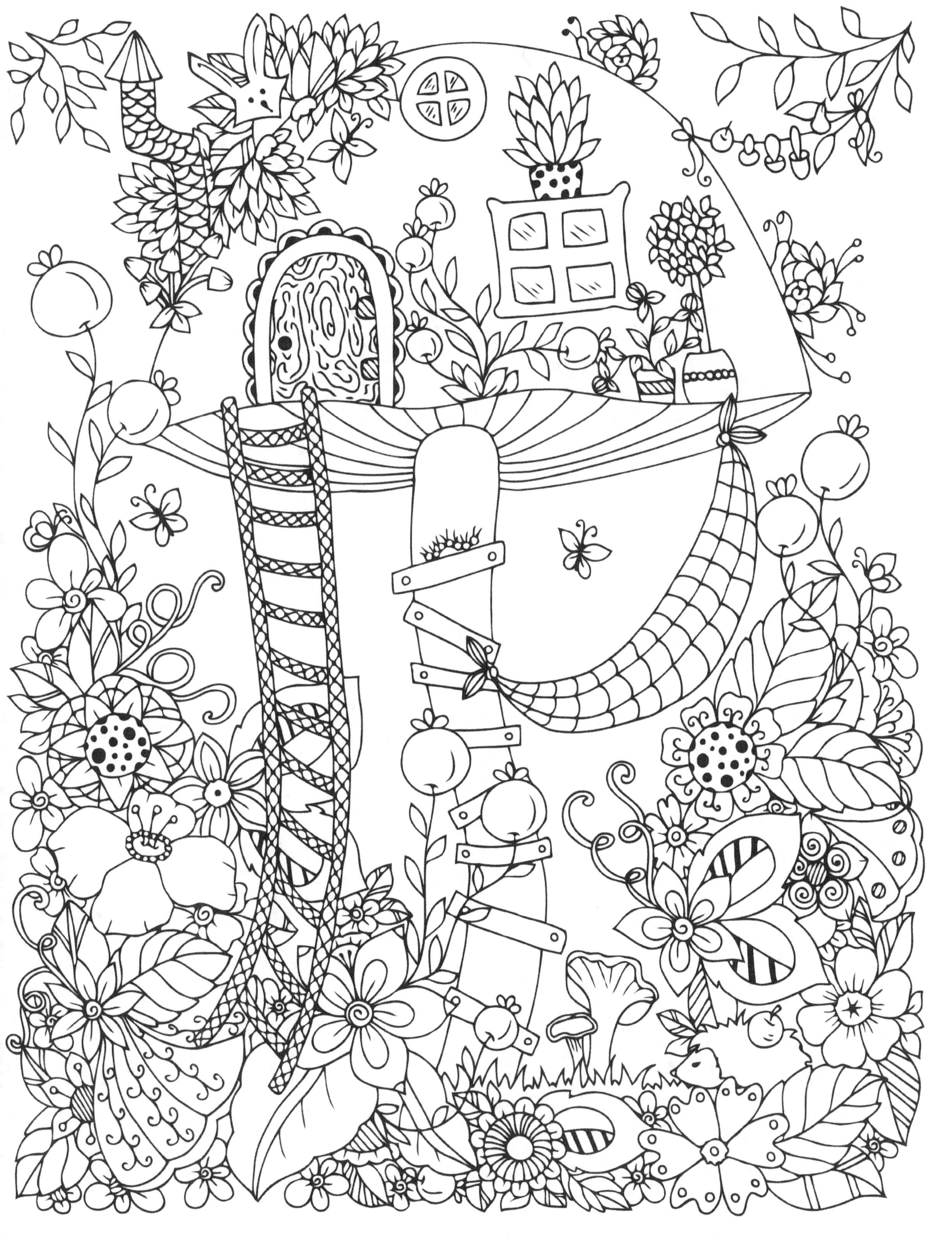

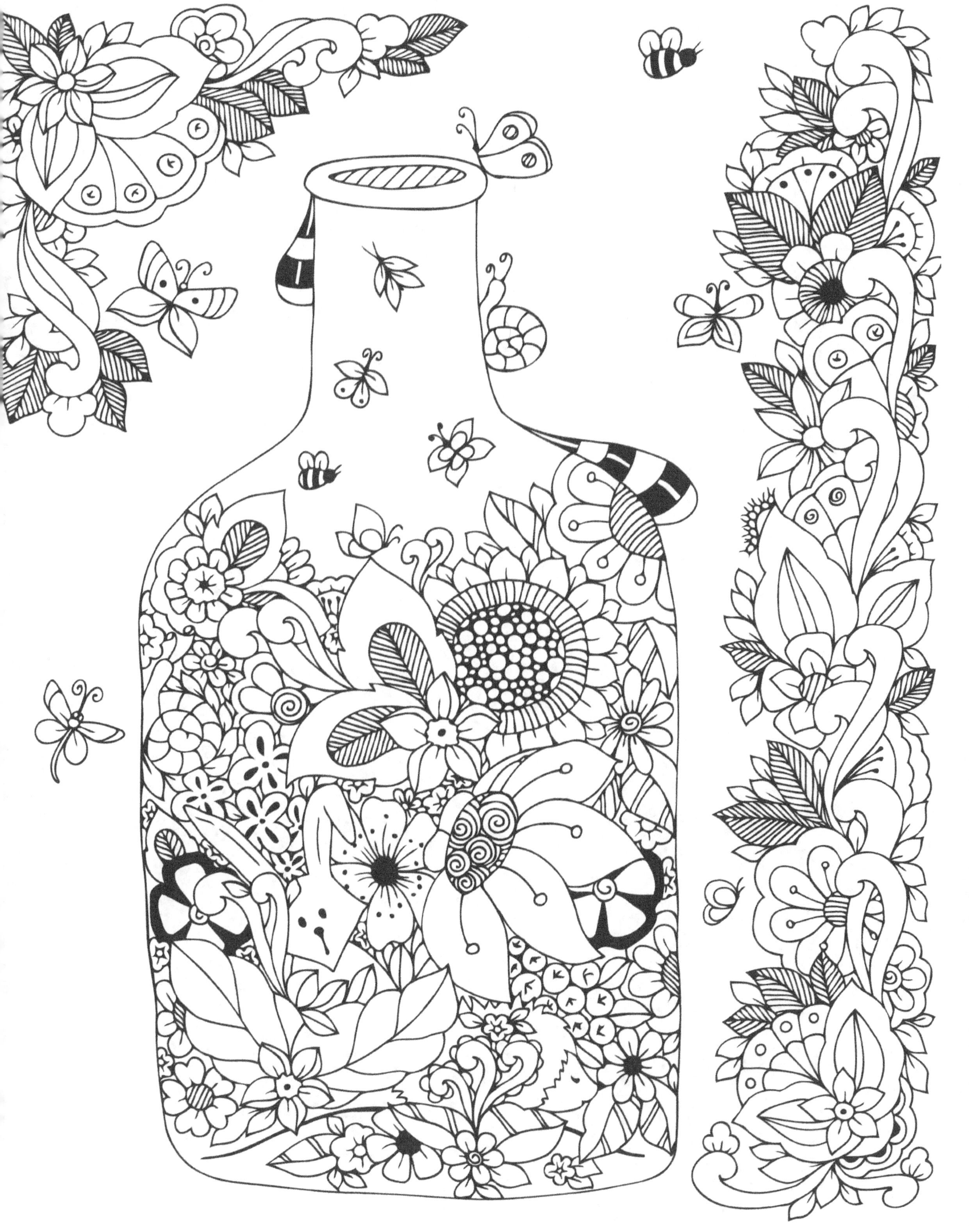

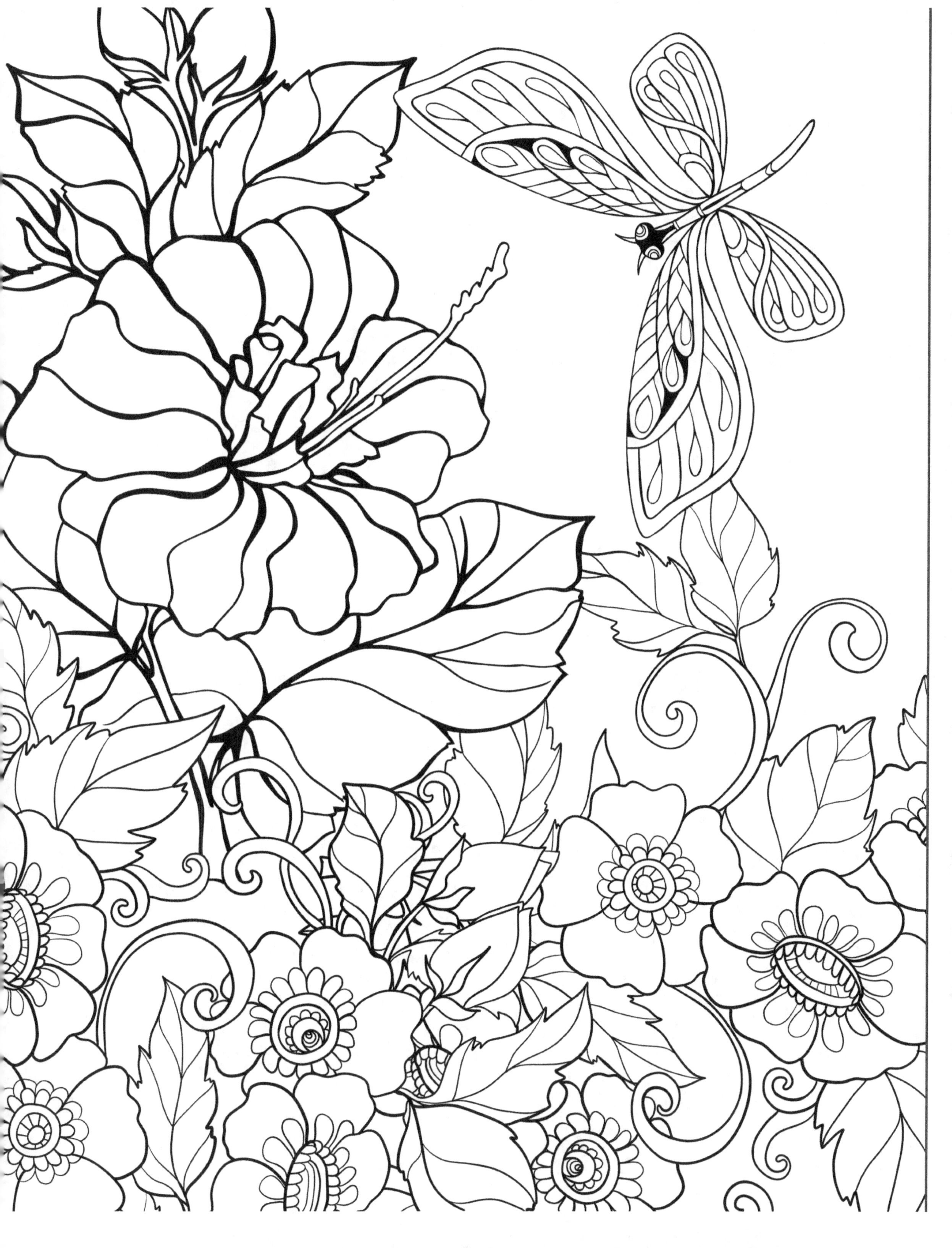

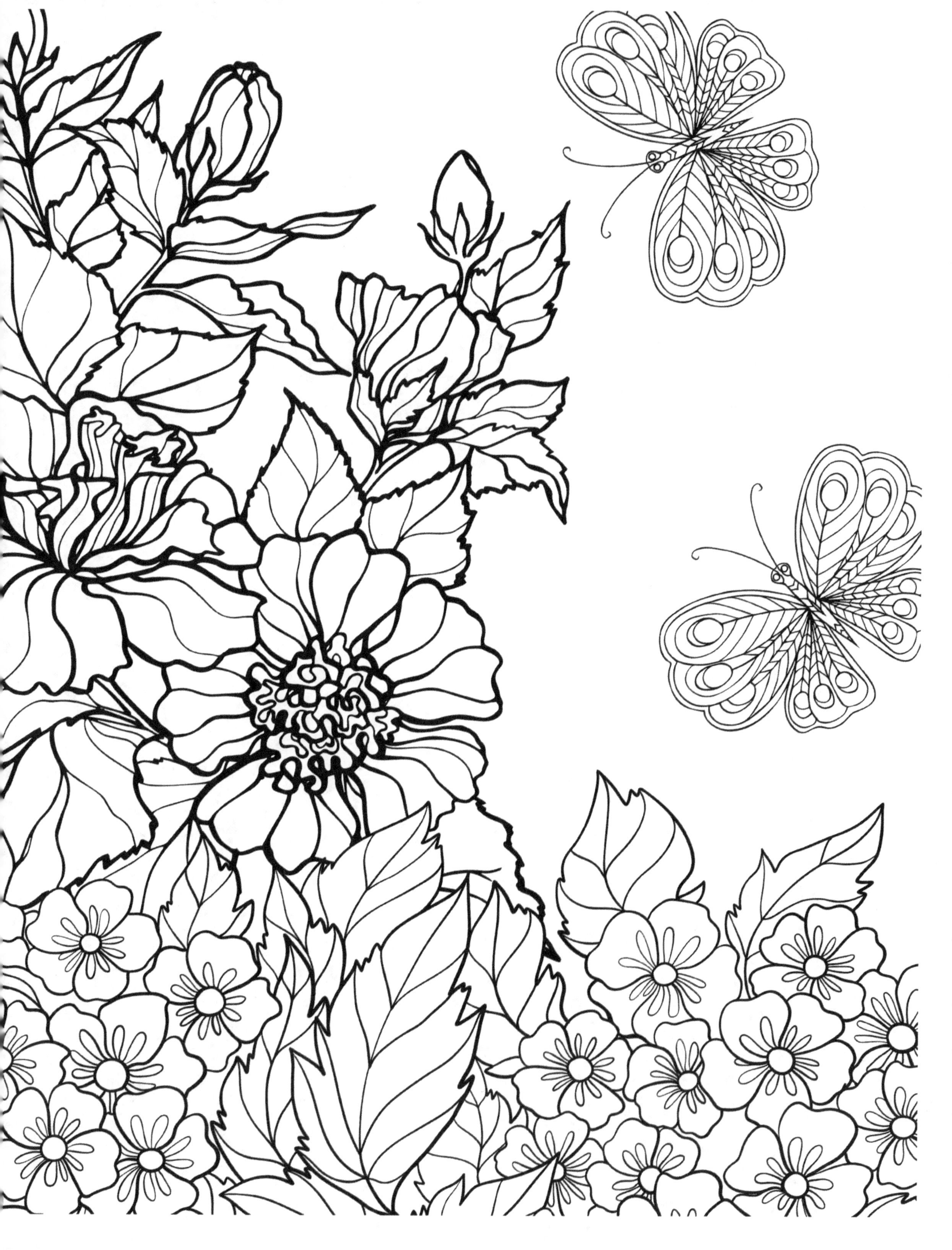

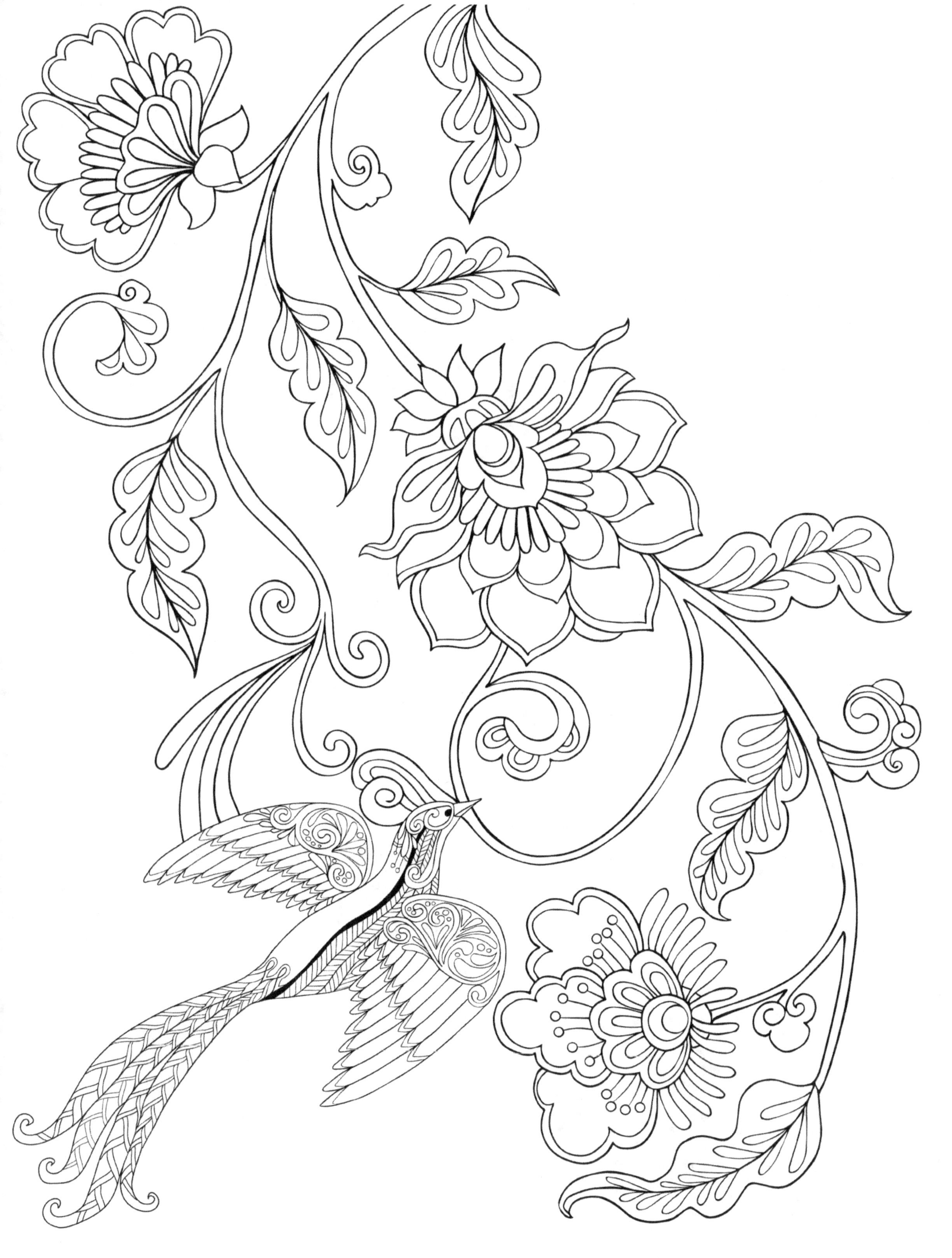

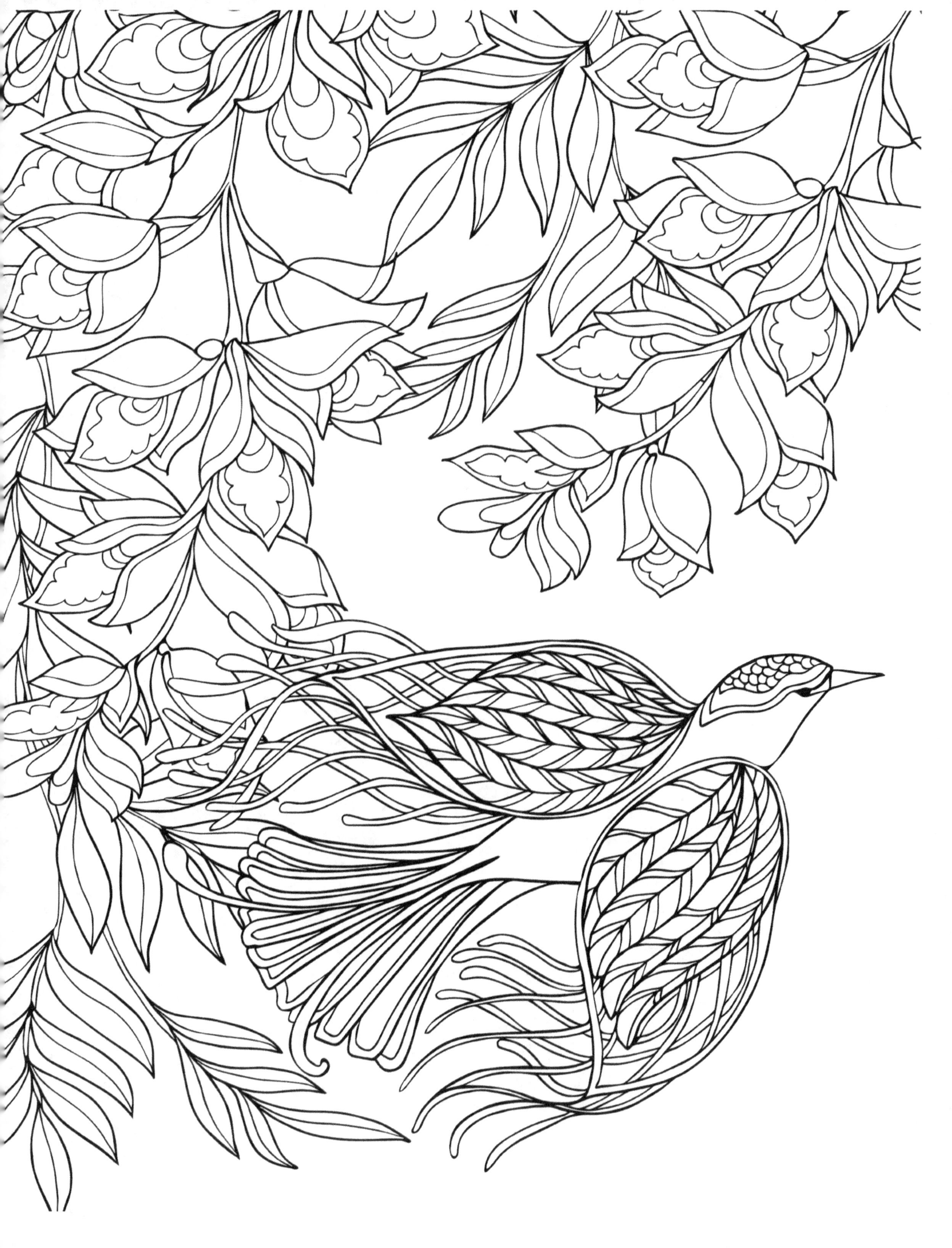

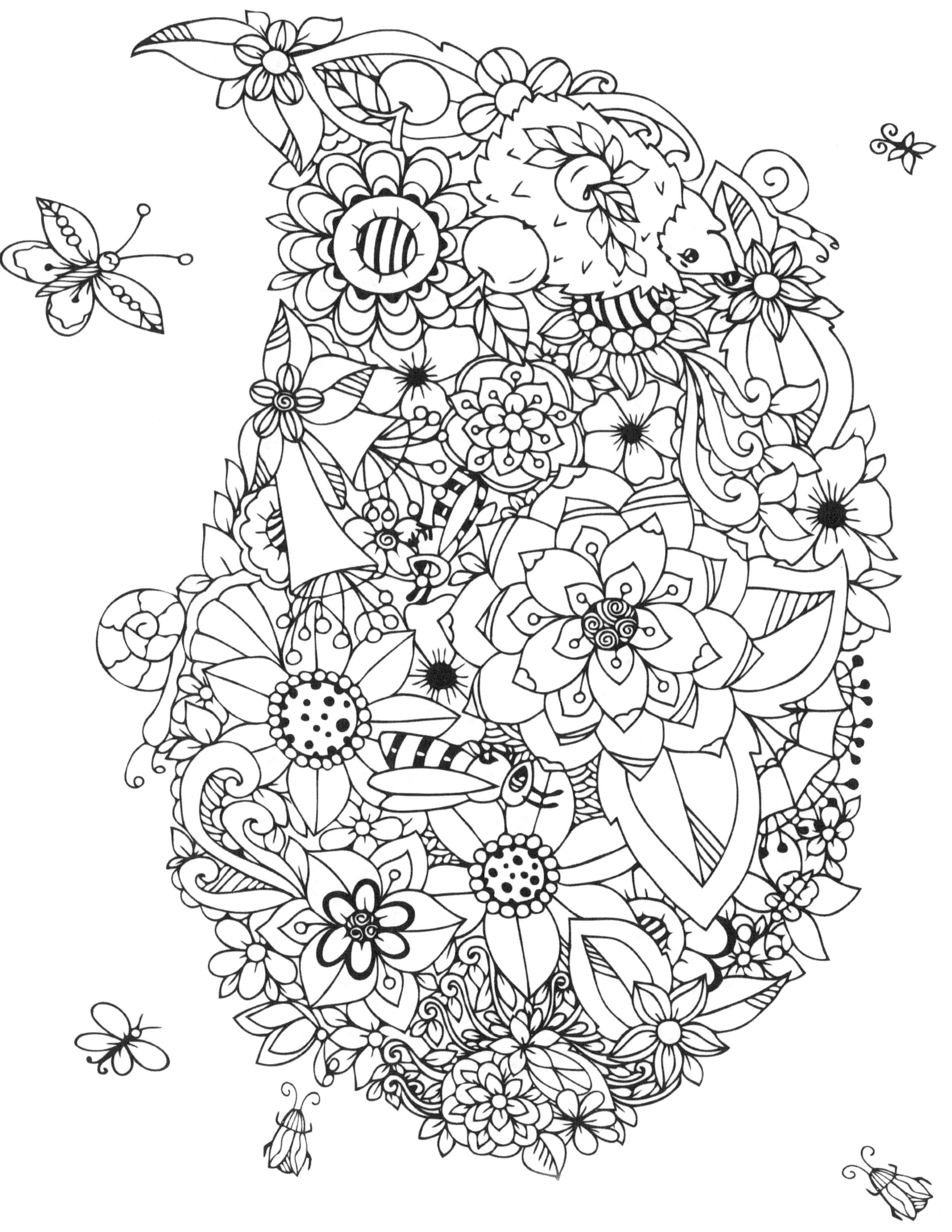

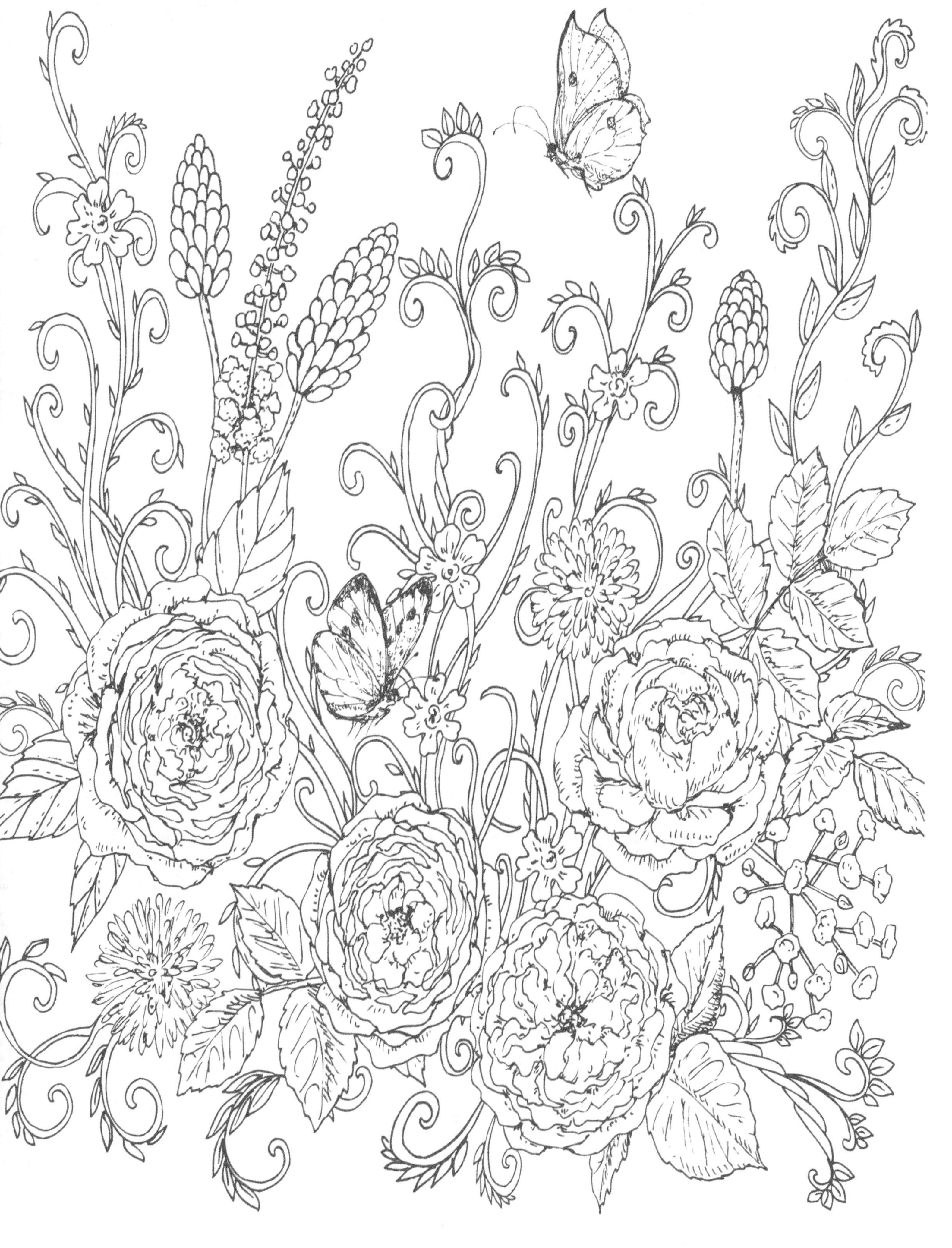

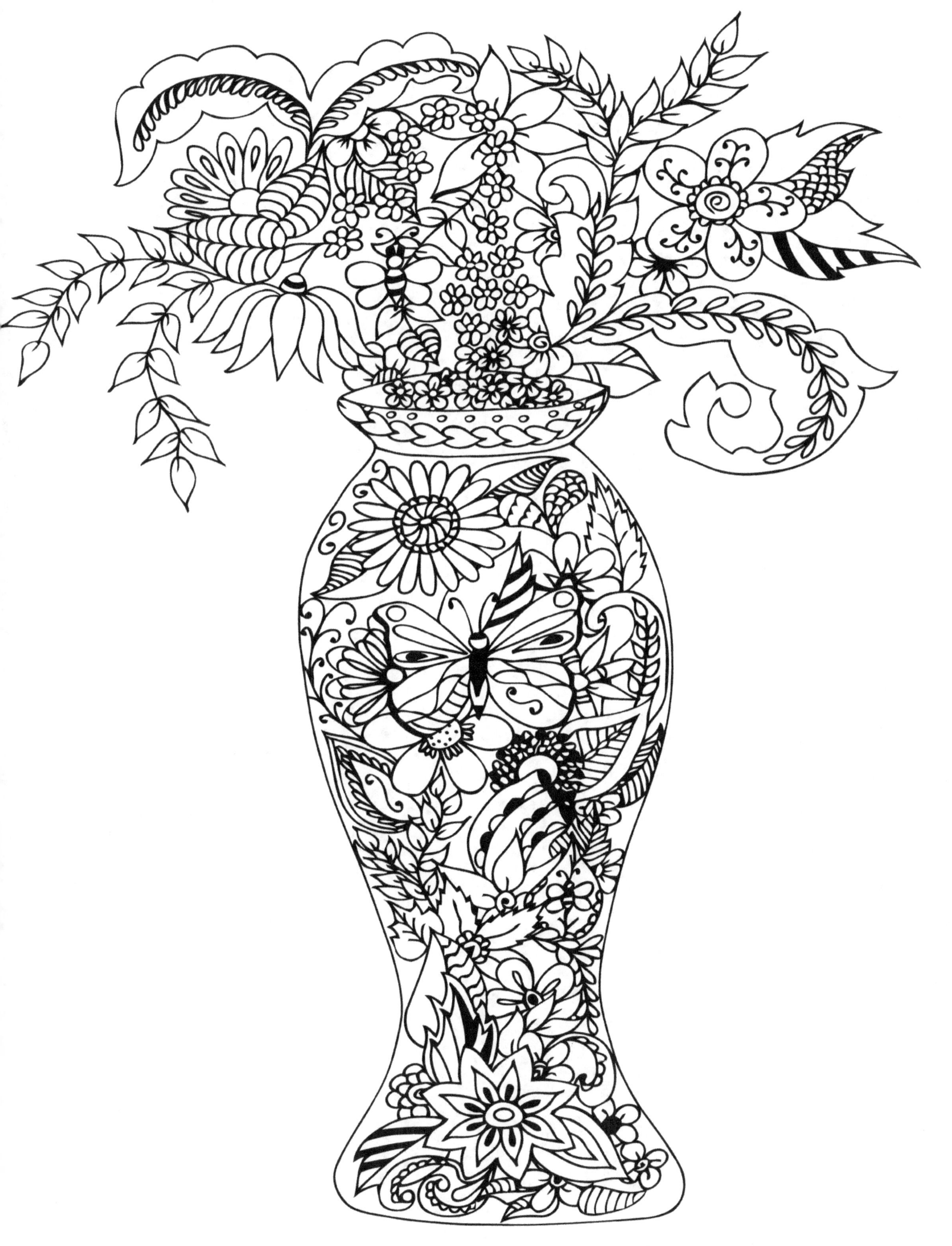

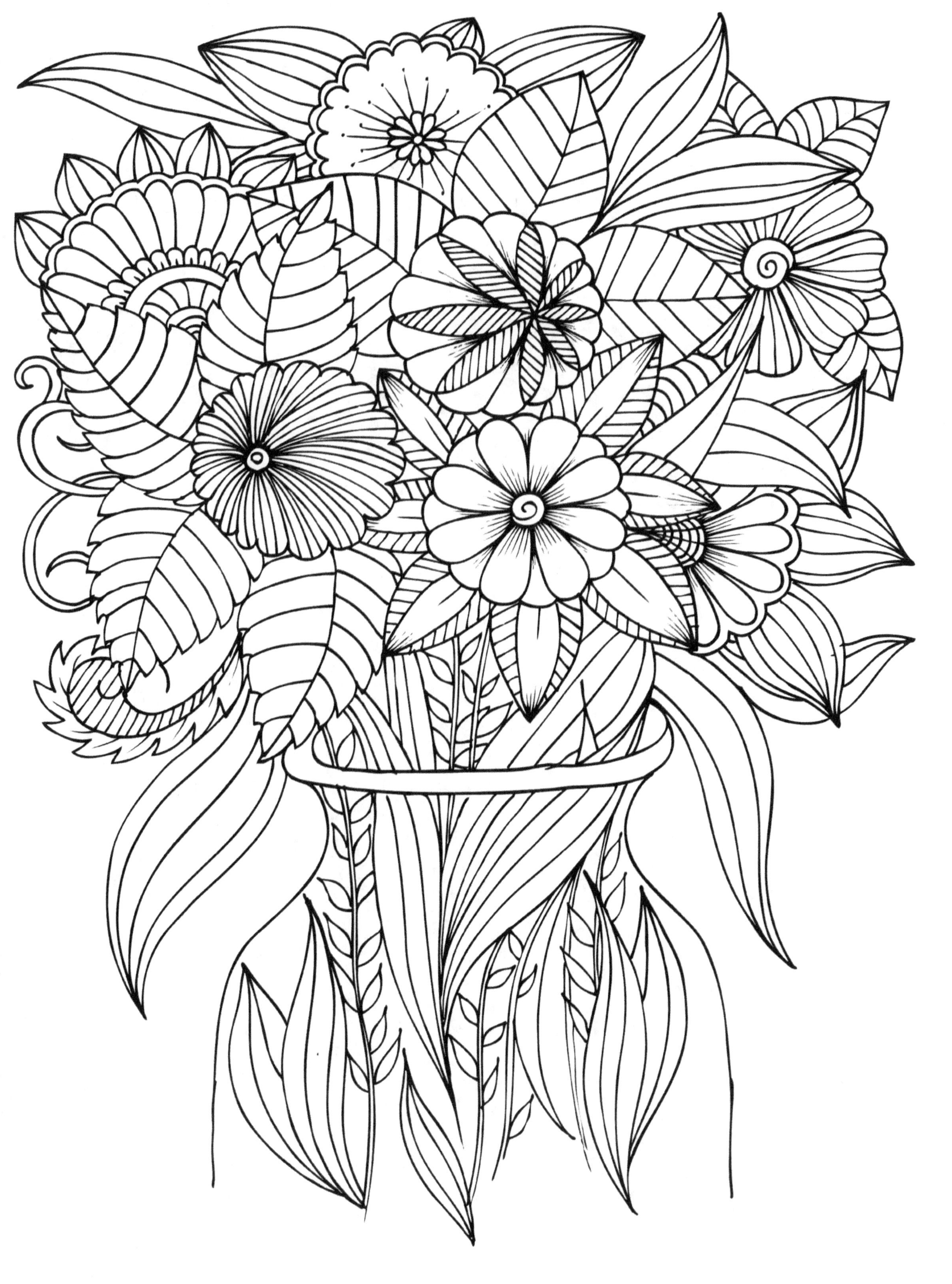

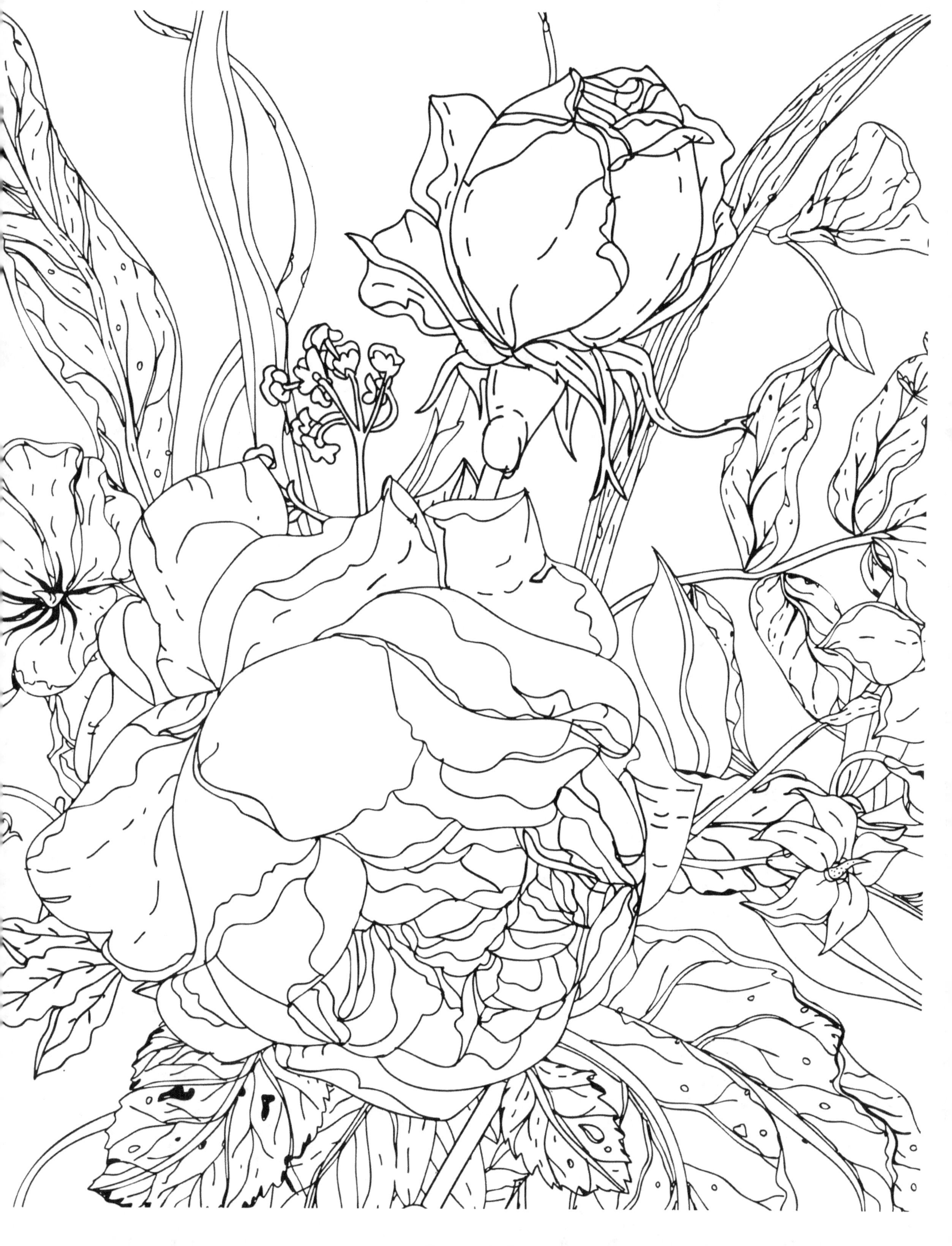